POETRY BASICS

VALERIE BODDEN

CREATIVE EDUCATION

Published by Creative Education
P.O. Box 227, Mankato, Minnesota 56002
Creative Education is an imprint of The Creative Company
www.thecreativecompany.us

Design and production by Stephanie Blumenthal
Printed by Corporate Graphics in the United States of America

Photographs by Alamy (Mary Evans Picture Library), Corbis (The Art Archive, Bettmann, Mary Iverson, Lake
Country Museum, Rykoff Collection, Stapleton Collection), Dreamstime (Andrzej5003), Getty Images
(Walter Langley, Edward Lear, Joe Munroe//Time & Life Pictures, William C. Shrout//Time & Life Pictures),
The Granger Collection, New York; iStockphoto (Nataliya Hora, Fuat Kose, Dr. Heinz Linke, Olga Rut\'ko),
Gary Kelley (page 6), Edward Lear, Nonsenselit.org

Library of Congress Cataloging-in-Publication Data
Bodden, Valerie.
Limericks / by Valerie Bodden.
p. cm. — (Poetry basics)
Includes bibliographical references and index.
ISBN 978-1-58341-777-5
1. Limericks, Juvenile. I. Title. II. Series.

PN6231.L5B52 2009
809.1'75—dc22   2008009159

6 8 9 7 5

People have written poems for thousands of years. Long ago, when people wanted to tell a story, they made it into a poem. Today, people write poems about all kinds of topics, from sunsets to traffic jams. Poems can help readers see things in a new way. They can make readers laugh or cry, sigh or scream. The goal of the type of poem known as a limerick is to present a humorous or **nonsense** situation in a short, rhyming verse.

No one knows exactly when the first limerick made the first reader chuckle in delight. Verses using the same rhyme and **rhythm** as modern limericks were written as long ago as the 1600s. But the word "limerick" wasn't used until the end of the 1800s, after the verse form had already become popular. (And no one knows for certain why "limerick" was chosen as a name for this type of poetry.)

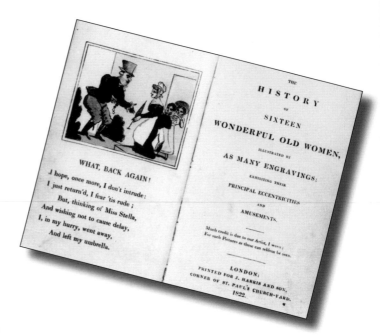

The first book consisting entirely of what are today called limericks was printed in 1820. *The History of Sixteen Wonderful Old Women*, by an unknown author, was published in England. The verses in this book, such as the one opposite, became very popular with children. In this verse, the word "pious" means "religious."

There was an Old Woman of Leeds,
Who spent all her time in Good Deeds,
She worked for the poor
Till her fingers were sore,
That pious Old Woman of Leeds.

Although additional limerick books were published over the next few years, the form didn't really take off until 1846. That year, *A Book of Nonsense* by Edward Lear came out. Lear was an artist who had been hired by England's **Earl** of Derby to illustrate a book. While working on the illustrations, Lear created a number of nonsense verses to amuse the earl's grandchildren. In Lear's verse on the next page, the word "repose" means "rest."

A Book of Nonsense was wildly successful, and children read and reread the verses until their copies of the book fell apart. Over the next 40 years, Lear continued to compose and publish nonsense verses.

There was an Old Man on whose nose

Most birds of the air would repose;

    But they all flew away

    At the closing of day,

Which relieved that Old Man and his nose.

PATRIOTISM IN EVERY SHOT.
(Copyright by "Judge," 1898.)

By the time Lear died in 1888, the limerick form had become popular throughout England and in America. Famous poets and **amateurs** alike enjoyed writing these brief, humorous verses. Soon, newspapers and companies began to hold limerick contests, in which contestants had to write one or more lines for a limerick. People competed for such prizes as money, homes, and horses.

Limericks briefly lost popularity during World War II, which lasted from 1939 to 1945. Although limerick-writing again took off after the war, limericks never again reached the level of prominence they had experienced during the early 1900s. Yet these short verses continue to be written and enjoyed today, and they still have the power to make readers of all ages smile.

Although limericks are short, they are not necessarily simple. Limericks are five-line poems that follow a definite form. They have a specific **rhyme scheme** and rhythm.

Words that rhyme end in the same sound. For example, "blue" rhymes with "clue," and "sleigh" rhymes with "hay." (Notice that rhyming words do not have to be spelled in the same way.) A limerick follows the rhyme scheme *aabba*. The letter *a* in the rhyme scheme stands for the first rhyming sound. So the last sounds of lines one, two, and five rhyme with each other. The letter *b* stands for the second rhyming sound. Lines three and four end with this sound. Pay attention to this rhyme scheme as you read the limerick on page 11 by American Gelett Burgess, written in 1914.

10

I wish that my room had a floor!
I don't care so much for a door,
But this crawling around
Without touching the ground,
Is getting to be quite a bore!

Part of the fun of reading limericks is listening to the way they sound. Rhyme makes up one part of a limerick's sound. Rhythm makes up another part. Rhythm in a poem is like the beat of a drum in a song. When we speak, we put a different amount of **stress** on different words or **syllables**. For example, try saying the word "simple" out loud. You probably said the first syllable with more force than the second syllable, so that it sounded like "SIM-ple."

Lines of poetry are divided into groups of syllables called feet. A foot is made up of one stressed syllable, along with one or two unstressed syllables. In a limerick, the first, second, and fifth lines usually have three feet. The third and fourth lines usually have two feet. Many limericks follow a "da DUM da da DUM da da DUM" rhythm in lines one, two, and five. Lines three and four usually follow either a "da DUM da da DUM" or a "da da DUM da da DUM" rhythm. In the next limerick by Edward Lear, the stressed syllables are printed in capital letters.

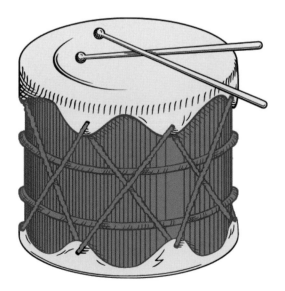

There WAS an old MAN with a BEARD,
Who SAID: "It is JUST as I FEARED!
  Two OWLS and a HEN,
  Four LARKS and a WREN,
Have ALL built their NESTS in my BEARD."

The use of alliteration also adds interest to the sound of some limericks. In alliteration, several words begin with the same letter or sound. For example, in the line "swiftly sledding over slippery snow," the "s" sound is repeated. Sometimes alliteration can even turn a limerick into a tongue twister, such as in the poem about Peter Piper on the opposite page.

Peter Piper picked a peck of pickled peppers.
A peck of pickled peppers Peter Piper picked.
If Peter Piper picked a peck of pickled peppers,
How many pickled peppers did Peter Piper pick?

LOTS OF LAUGHS

Limericks were some of the first verses printed simply to amuse children. Unlike earlier children's books, which were meant to serve as teaching tools, books of limericks were intended purely for entertainment. Although "dirty" limericks have been written since the poetry form was first developed, good, clean humor is still the basis for many of the most enduring limericks.

Most limericks begin with a line about a person, often referred to simply as "a man" or "a woman." The first line of a limerick also often ends by saying where that person is from. In fact, part of the challenge of limerick writing can be thinking of words to rhyme with a place name, as in the example on page 18 from the 1822 book *Anecdotes and Adventures of Fifteen Gentlemen*, believed to have been written by an English grocer named Richard Scrafton Sharpe. In this limerick, the person is from Quebec, Canada.

The second, third, and fourth lines of a limerick provide the "plot." They tell what the person introduced in the first line does. In the verse below, the tailor (a person who makes clothes) goes onto the deck of a ship during a storm. The final line of some limericks simply restates the first line of the verse. But the last line of many other limericks shows what ultimately happens to the person. Often, this line presents a twist that surprises the reader—and brings on a laugh!

A Tailor, who sailed from Quebec,
In a storm ventur'd once upon deck;
    But the waves of the sea
    Were as strong as could be,
And he tumbled in up to his neck.

Part of the humor of many limericks is that they are nonsense. They are about things that could not really happen. For example, the limerick below by Edward Lear presents a nonsense situation.

There was a young lady whose chin
Resembled the point of a pin;
    So she had it made sharp,
    And purchased a harp,
And played several tunes with her chin.

Throughout its history, the limerick has been used to cover a wide range of topics. Limericks have been written about politics, religion, and **philosophy.** They have been written about real and imaginary people, animals, and plants. Limericks about sports, music, and schools have also been written. Even math and science have been the topics of limericks!

O ften, limericks deal with current events. So reading limericks can help readers see what was important to people during a specific time in history. For example, during World War I (1914–18), many limericks were written about Kaiser Wilhelm II, the leader of Germany.

MORE NONSENSE

Although limericks are well known for their nonsense, they are not the only kind of nonsense poems. Poets have used many different forms to write nonsense verses over the years. But just because a poem is funny does not mean that it is nonsense. Some funny poems make sense. Nonsense verses, like many limericks, are about things that could not really happen. As you read the verse on the next page by 20th-century American poet Hughes Mearns, think about why it is nonsense.

As I was going up the stair
I saw a man who wasn't there.
Hc wasn't there again today
I wish, I wish he'd stay away.

Sometimes nonsense verses make use of nonsense words. The words are not simply gibberish, though. They are part of a made-up language. As you read them, you get the feeling that if you understood the language, you would understand the poem.

Some nonsense poems are made up of both real and nonsense words. Often the nonsense words in a nonsense poem are nonce (*NONS*) words. Nonce words are words that are invented to be used once for a specific need.

A few of the words in a nonsense poem might also be portmanteau (*port-MAN-toh*) words. Portmanteau words are made by combining the sounds and meanings of two different words. For example, "smog" is a portmanteau word made from "smoke" and "fog," and "brunch" is a combination of "breakfast" and "lunch."

The nonsense poem "Jabberwocky" appears in English author Lewis Carroll's 1871 book *Through the Looking-Glass and What Alice Found There*. In the book, the character Humpty Dumpty explains the meaning of some of the poem's portmanteau words. He says that "slithy" is a combination of "slimy" and "lithe" (a word meaning active and graceful). As you read the part of the poem printed on the opposite page, see if you can identify any other portmanteau words.

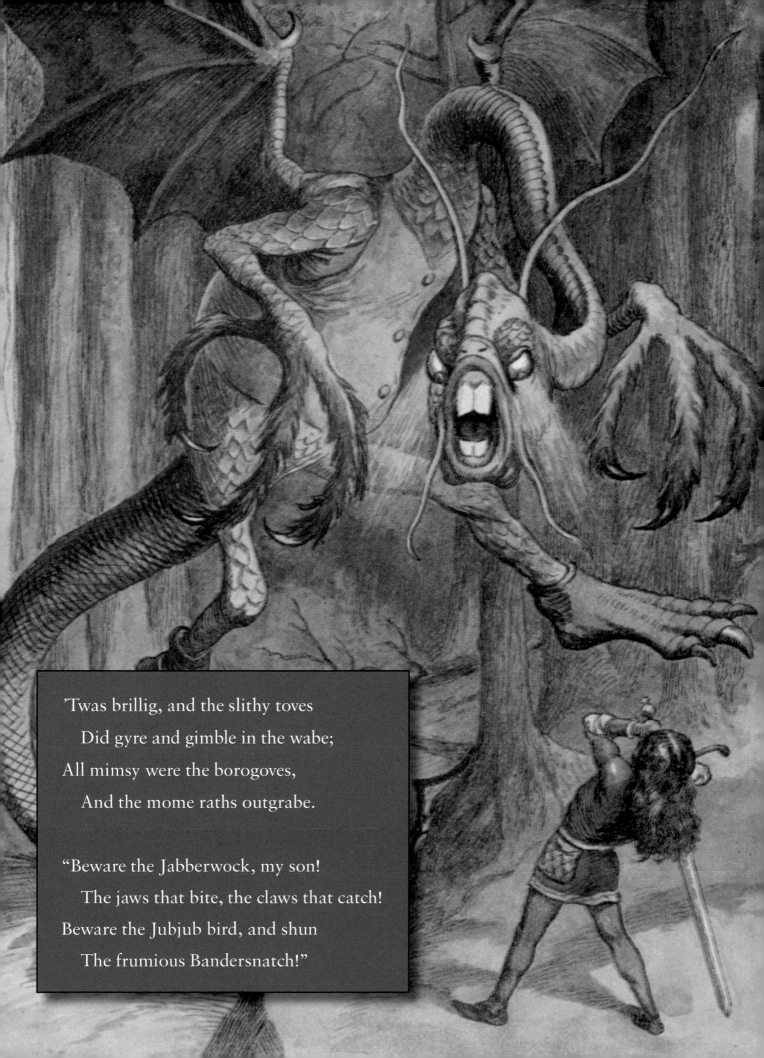

’Twas brillig, and the slithy toves
   Did gyre and gimble in the wabe;
All mimsy were the borogoves,
   And the mome raths outgrabe.

“Beware the Jabberwock, my son!
   The jaws that bite, the claws that catch!
Beware the Jubjub bird, and shun
   The frumious Bandersnatch!”

Whether you're reading nonsense poems or limericks, you're likely to be smiling. You might even be laughing out loud! Along with your laughter, you might find yourself getting caught up in the rhyme and rhythm of limericks. And after reading limericks, the rhyme scheme and rhythm of other types of poems might be easier for you to spot, which can add new levels of meaning to poetry.

THINK LIKE A POET

1. *Your personal limerick.* Write a limerick about yourself. First, think of all the words that rhyme with your first (or last) name. Make your first line something like, "There was a young fellow named Jim." Now, write the rest of the limerick, being sure that lines two and five rhyme with your name. Try to follow the rhythm of a limerick, too. And make it as silly as you want it to be!

2. *A new twist.* It can be fun to put a new twist on an old limerick. Choose one of the limericks in this book. Write a new limerick using the same first line as the old limerick. Try to use a completely different idea from that of the original limerick, though. For example, if you decide to write about Edward Lear's old man with a beard, try to make the limerick about something other than birds making their homes in the beard.

Ciardi, John. *The Hopeful Trout and Other Limericks*. Boston: Houghton Mifflin, 1989.

Lear, Edward. *A Book of Nonsense*. New York: Alfred A. Knopf, 1992.

Livingston, Myra Cohn. *Lots of Limericks*. New York: M. K. McElderry, 1991.

Tripp, Wallace, comp. *Rose's Are Red, Violet's Are Blue: And Other Silly Poems*. Boston: Little, Brown and Company, 1999.

GLOSSARY

amateurs—people who do an activity for fun and not because it's their job

earl—a title for a man in a high position in English society

nonsense—lacking meaning or not making sense

philosophy—the study of the meaning behind such things as truth, reality, and freedom

rhyme scheme—the pattern of rhymes in a poem; a rhyme scheme shows which lines rhyme with which other lines

rhythm—the pattern of sounds or stresses in a line of poetry

stress—emphasis; words given more stress are said louder or with more force than other words

syllables—complete units of sound that make up words; for example "sit" has one syllable, and "si-lent" has two

BIBLIOGRAPHY

Bibby, Cyril. *The Art of the Limerick*. Hamden, Conn.: Archon Books, 1978.

Harrowven, Jean. *The Limerick Makers*. London: Research Publishing Co., 1976.

Livingston, Myra Cohn. *How Pleasant to Know Mr. Lear*. New York: Holiday House, 1982.

McGraw, H. Ward, ed. *Prose and Poetry for Enjoyment*. Chicago: L. W. Singer Co., 1935.

Parrott, E. O., ed. *The Penguin Book of Limericks*. New York: Penguin Books, 1983.

Reed, Langford. *The Complete Limerick Book*. New York: G. P. Putnam's Sons, 1925.

INDEX

alliteration 14

America 8

Burgess, Gelett 10, 11
  "I Wish That My Room Had a Floor!" 11

Carroll, Lewis 26, 27
  "Jabberwocky" 26, 27

early limericks 4, 6, 16
  publications of 4, 6, 16

England 4, 6, 8

Lear, Edward 6, 7, 8, 12, 13, 19, 29
  A Book of Nonsense 6
  "There Was an Old Man on Whose Nose" 7
  "There Was an Old Man with a Beard" 13, 29
  "There Was a Young Lady Whose Chin" 19

limerick contests 8

limerick structure 10, 12, 14, 17–18

Mearns, Hughes 22, 23
  "As I Was Going up the Stair" 23

nonce words 25

nonsense 3, 6, 19, 22, 24, 25, 28

poetic feet 12

popularity with children 4, 6, 8

portmanteau words 25, 26

rhyme 4, 12, 17, 28, 29

rhyme schemes 10, 28

rhyming words 10, 17

rhythm 4, 10, 12, 28, 29
  and stress 12
  and syllables 12

Sharpe, Richard Scrafton 17
  Anecdotes and Adventures of Fifteen Gentlemen 17

subjects 20–21

"There Was an Old Woman of Leeds" 5

tongue twisters 14

verses 3, 4, 6, 8, 16, 18, 22, 24

World War I 21

World War II 8